JERRY'S GIRLS

A Musical Revue
starring

The Music and Lyrics of
Jerry Herman
Concept by Jerry Herman and *I   'ford*

SAMUEL FRENCH, INC.
25 WEST 45TH STREET   NEW YORK 10036
7623 SUNSET BOULEVARD   HOLLYWOOD 90046
LONDON   TORONTO

Amateurs wishing to arrange for the production of JERRY'S GIRLS must make application to SAMUEL FRENCH, INC., at 25 West 45th Street, New York, N.Y. 10036, giving the following particulars:

(1) The name of the town and theatre or hall in which it is proposed to give the production.
(2) The maximum seating capacity of the theatre or hall.
(3) Scale of ticket prices.
(4) The number of performances it is intended to give, and the dates thereof.
(5) The title, number of performances, gross receipts and amount of royalty and rental paid on your last musical performed.

Upon receipt of these particulars SAMUEL FRENCH, INC., will quote the amateur terms and availability.

MUSICAL NUMBERS

PART ONE

"Jerry's Girls" ("It's Today"/ *Mame*)................The Girls
OPTIMIST MEDLEY:
   "Put On Your Sunday Clothes"/ *Hello, Dolly!* ....Girl 2
   "Open A New Window"/ *Mame*..................The Girls
   "Chin Up Ladies"/ *Milk and Honey* ....The Girls
"It Only Takes A Moment"/ *Hello, Dolly!* ....Girl 4
"Wherever He Ain't"/ *Mack and Mabel* ....Girl 1
"We Need A Little Christmas"/ *Mame* ..'............The Girls
"I Won't Send Roses"/ *Mack and Mabel*................Girl 3
"Tap Your Troubles Away"/ *Mack and Mabel*..........Girl 1
VAUDEVILLE MEDLEY:
   "Two-A-Day"/ *Parade* ....Girl 4
   "Bosom Buddies"/ *Mame* ....Girls 3, 2
   "I Wanna Make The World Laugh"/
     Mack and Mabel ....Girl 1
   "The Man In The Moon"/ *Mame*.................The Girls
   "So Long Dearie"/ *Hello, Dolly!* ....Girl 4
   "Two-A-Day" (reprise) ....The Girls
"If He Walked Into My Life"/ *Mame* ....Girl 2
"Hello, Dolly!" ....The Girls

INTERMISSION

PART TWO

MOVIES MEDLEY:
   "Just Go To The Movies"/ *A Day In Hollywood,*
     A Night In The Ukraine ....The Girls
   "Movies Were Movies"/ Mack and Mabel.............Girl 4
   "Look What Happened To Mabel"/
     Mack and Mabel ....Girl 1
   "Nelson"/ *Hollywood, Ukraine* ....Girl 3
   "Just Go To The Movies" (reprise) ....The Girls
"Shalom"/ *Milk and Honey* ....Girl 2
"Milk and Honey" ....The Girls
"Time Heals Everything"/ *Mack and Mabel*............Girl 1
"Mame" ....The Girls
"Kiss Her Now"/ *Dear World* ....Girls 2, 4
"The Tea Party"/ *Dear World:* Dickie..................Girl 1
                       Voices..................Girl 3
                       Thoughts ....Girl 2

All music published by E.H. Morris/MPL, except *The Grand
Tour* by G. Schirmer, Inc.

CAST
(In order of appearance)

ALEXANDRA KOREY
LEILA MARTIN
EVALYN BARON
PUALETTA PEARSON

Musical Direction
CHERYL HARDWICK

Set and Lighting Design   Costume Design
HAL TINÉ   BERNARD JOHNSON

Choreography   Choral Arrangements   Photography
SHARON HALLEY   JOHN VISSER   MARTHA SWOPE
PHIL HALL

Musical Arrangements
JERRY HERMAN

Production Stage Managers
GENE BLAND
TODD FLEISCHER

Casting by MARK REINER of Contemporary Casting

Staged and Directed by
LARRY ALFORD

Presented by

The Bosom Buddies Company
at Ted Hook's Onstage, NYC

NOTES TO THE DIRECTOR

JERRY'S GIRLS is a musical revue that celebrates the music and lyrics of award-winning Broadway composer Jerry Herman. And since some of the best songs Mr. Herman has written for his major shows (HELLO, DOLLY!, MAME, DEAR WORLD, and MACK AND MABEL) were written for and about women, it is fitting that the cast and orchestra for JERRY'S GIRLS are female.

The revue's staging is based on concepts that are original, yet simple and that affectionately honor Jerry Herman's special mixture of famous show-stoppers, ballads, and comedy songs.

From start to finish this is an evening that one critic called "an entertainment bonanza of melodic, winning musical theatre." And it can be the same for your production.

JERRY'S GIRLS is a theatrical/presentational revue, and you should avoid recreating actual moments from the various shows. All of those involved in creating this revue believe that Jerry Herman's songs have lives of their own outside the theatre. With JERRY'S GIRLS we have tried to present new, simple creations and not "carbon copies."

Best wishes for a successful production.

—LARRY ALFORD

Jerry's Girls

PART ONE

House to half
IT'S TODAY fanfare
Star portraits lit as house fades
J.G.#1 enters US.L.*, gestures to Channing portrait and sings:*

J.G.#1.
CAROL CHANNING
BEATRICE ARTHUR
ETHEL MERMAN
JERRY'S GIRLS!

(steps to second platform and continues)

THERE'S PEARL BAILEY AND BERNADETTE PETERS
ANGELA LANSBURY DOUBLED HER FAME
(gestures to Lansbury portrait)
THE WINTER GARDEN WAS SELL OUT
WHEN SHE PLAYED THE HELL OUT OF MAME!

(Freezes in stylized "MAME" bugle pose for a moment, then
observes J.G.#2 who enters and sings:)

J.G.#2.
PHYLLIS DILLER
PHYLLIS NEWMAN
ANNIE MILLER
DOIN' TWIRLS
(does dance twirl and moves DS.C.*)*

LISA KIRK IN "MACK AND MABEL"
GINGER ROGERS, BETTY GRABLE
(does famous Grable pin-up pose)
ARE JUST SOME OF
(J.G.#1 joins J.G.#2 at piano as they sing in harmony.)
JERRY'S GIRLS!

7

(*J.G.#3 enters* US.R. *and sings:*)

J.G.#3.
(*sultry pose*)
SUSAN HAYWARD
(*goofy*)
DODY GOODMAN
(*with great innocence*)
MARY MARTIN
JERRY'S GIRLS!

(*moves* D.C. *toward piano*)

HE'S HAD LUCIE ARNAZ AND HER MOTHER
AND JANIS PAIGE, JANET BLAIR, MARTHA RAYE,
MIMI BENZELL WOOING WEEDE,
CELESTE HOLM AND EYDIE GORME!
(*leans against piano*)

(*J.G.#4 enters* US.L. *and sings:*)

J.G.#4.
EILEEN BRENNAN
IN HER RIBBONS
(*flutters imaginary ribbons*)
KITTY CARLYLE
IN HER PEARLS
(*moves* DS.L)

VERA CHARLES AND CLARA WEISS AND
MOLLY PICON, BARBRA STREISAND
(*profile*)
ARE SOME MORE OF JERRY'S GIRLS!

(*All four sing as they move together* DS.L. *Girls dance* S.R. *as
they sing:*)

THERE'S MISS GINGOLD
AND MISS SOTHERN
AND MISS ARDEN
AND MISS PROWSE
(*J.G.#4 does Juliet Prowse "legs" pose.*)
J.G.#2.
HE'S HAD DOTTIE LAMOUR AND JANE RUSSELL

J.G.#3.
AND ERNISTINA AND HER HOOTCHY KOOTCH
(*shakes her bosom*)
　J.G.#1.
HE'S HAD MISS SWITT
　J.G.#4.
AND MISS STRICH
　J.G.#2.
AND MISS SYMS
　J.G.#3.
AND MISS COOK
　ALL.
AND MISS GOOCH!

(*Girls move together as they sing:*)

MRS. LEVI
MOTHER BURNSIDE
MABEL NORMAND
IN HER CURLS
(*All lean together for a movie close-up pose.*)

OH THE MARQUEES
(*All indicate star portraits.*)
THEY'VE IGNITED
WE'RE ECSTATIC
AND EXCITED
TO BE SOME OF
JERRY'S GIRLS!

(*On final chord of music, all ladies strike a star pose: i.e. Ann Miller, Grable, Lansbury/MAME and Prowse/'legs'. JERRY'S GIRLS playoff, all but J.G.#2 exit.*)

SUNDAY CLOTHES (*with quiet charm*)

(*She takes a hat and parasol from piano. As she sings, others enter with hats and parasols and freeze.*)

　J.G.#2.
PUT ON YOUR SUNDAY CLOTHES WHEN YOU FEEL
　DOWN AND OUT

STRUT DOWN THE STREET AND HAVE YOUR PICTURE
    TOOK;
(*On music cue, all do Gibson Girl portrait pose.*)
DRESSED LIKE A DREAM YOUR SPIRITS SEEM TO
    TURN ABOUT

THAT SUNDAY SHINE
IS A CERTAIN SIGN
THAT YOU FEEL AS FINE AS YOU LOOK

BENEATH YOUR PARASOL, THE WORLD IS ALL A
    SMILE
(*All open parasols slowly.*)
THAT MAKES YOU FEEL BRAND NEW DOWN TO YOUR
    TOES;

GET OUT YOUR FEATHERS
YOUR PATENT LEATHERS
YOUR BEADS AND BUCKLES AND BOWS
    ALL.
FOR THERE'S NO BLUE MONDAY
IN YOUR SUNDAY CLOTHES.

(*Cast whistles and moves* DS.C. *to create a parasol semi-circle.*)

    ALL.
OPEN A NEW WINDOW
OPEN A NEW DOOR
TRAVEL A NEW HIGHWAY
THAT'S NEVER BEEN TRIED BEFORE . . .

        CHIN UP, LADIES (militant, marshal)

    ALL.
HUP, HUP
(*close parasols and use as marching batons*)
CHIN UP, LADIES!
LOOK BEYOND THE HORIZON
HEADS HIGH, LADIES!
DON'T GIVE UP THE SHIP

(*Girl #3 becomes drill sergeant with other ladies "falling in
    line" for exercises, etc.*)

LOOK FOR THE SILVER LINING
YA GOTTA GO ON WITH THE SHOW
CLIMB EVERY MOUNTAIN
TO FIND YOUR MR. SNOW

AND ALWAYS A HIP-HUP, LADIES!
THERE'S A BRIGHTER TOMORROW
STIFF UPPER LIP UP, LADIES!
DO OR DIE IS THE PLAN

WHEN THE TRIP IS OVER
TO PROVE THAT WE WERE HERE
WE'D LIKE TO CARRY HOME
(*All cradle umbrellas like babies.*)
A SIX-FOOT SOUVENIR!

SO KEEP YOUR CHIN UP, LADIES!
SOMEWHERE OVER THE RAINBOW
THERE'S A MAN!

(*with the spirit of cheerleaders*)
WITH A VEE-VO, AND A VIE-VO
AND A VEE-VO VIE-VO VUM
WITH A CHEER UP AND A CLEAR UP
AND A DON'T BE, WON'T BE GLUM

WITH A SMILE WHENEVER YOU'RE ABLE
AND A LAUGH WHENEVER YOU CAN
'CAUSE, LADIES
SOMEWHERE OVER THE RAINBOW
THERE'S A MAN!

(*With mounting excitement the music builds as the women open
     parasols and twirl them like train wheels.*)

BENEATH YOUR PARASOL THE WORLD IS ALL A
     SMILE
THAT MAKES YOU FEEL BRAND NEW DOWN TO YOUR
     TOES
GET OUT YOUR FEATHERS
YOUR PATENT LEATHER
YOUR BEADS AND BUCKLES AND BOWS

IN YOUR NEW STRAW HAT
AND YOUR SILK CRAVAT
THERE'LL BE NO BLUE MONDAY
IN YOUR SUNDAY CLOTHES
(*Repeat Gibson Girl pose.*)

(*Girls, except #4, move offstage in easy slow motion as they sing
    in harmony, quietly and romantically:*)

NO WE WON'T COME HOME
NO WE WON'T COME HOME
NO WE WON'T COME HOME
UNTIL WE FALL IN LOVE

IT ONLY TAKES A MOMENT

(*J.G.#4 removes her hat, holds it and sings tenderly and hushed:*)
IT ONLY TAKES A MOMENT
FOR YOUR EYES TO MEET, AND THEN
YOUR HEART KNOWS IN A MOMENT
YOU WILL NEVER BE ALONE AGAIN

I HELD HIM, FOR AN INSTANT
BUT HIS ARMS FELT SAFE AND STRONG
IT ONLY TAKES A MOMENT
TO BE LOVED A WHOLE LIFE LONG

(*passionately*)
HE HELD ME, FOR AN INSTANT
BUT HIS ARMS FELT SURE AND STRONG
IT ONLY TAKES A MOMENT
TO BE LOVED A WHOLE LIFE LONG
(*hushed again*)
AND THAT IS ALL
THAT LOVE'S ABOUT
AND WE'LL RECALL
WHEN TIME RUNS OUT

THAT IT ONLY TOOK A MOMENT
TO BE LOVED A WHOLE LIFE LONG

(*J.G.#4 exits during staccato intro, as J.G.#1 enters* U.L. *wearing a period hat and carrying a suitcase. She drops it on cue and sings:*)

WHEREVER HE AIN'T *(with defiance)*

J.G.#1.
I GOTTA GIVE MY LIFE SOME SPARKLE AND FIZZ
AND THINK A THOUGHT THAT ISN'T WRAPPED UP
   IN HIS
THE PLACE THAT I CONSIDER PARADISE IS
WHEREVER HE AIN'T!
WHEREVER HE AIN'T!

(*picks up suitcase*)

NO MORE TO WITHER WHEN HE'S GROUCHY AND
   GRUFF
NO MORE TO LISTEN TO HIM BELLOW AND BLUFF
TOMORROW MORNING I'LL BE STRUTTIN' MY STUFF
WHEREVER HE AIN'T!
WHEREVER HE AIN'T!

(*moves* DS.R.)

ENOUGH OF BEING BULLIED AND BOSSED
TA-TA, AUF WEIDERSEHN AND GET LOST!

I WALKED BEHIND HIM LIKE A MEEK LITTLE LAMB
AND HAD MY FILL OF HIS NOT GIVING A DAMN
I'LL GO TO SYDNEY, OR CEYLON, OR SIAM
WHEREVER HE AIN'T!
WHEREVER HE AIN'T!

(*Looks back toward entrance* U.L., *moves as if to return to "him", but decides differently and starts to exit. However, she turns back to exclaim!*)

IT'S TIME FOR LITTLE NELL TO REBEL
IF HE'S IN HEAVEN, I'LL GO TO HELL!

(*puts down suitcase and sits*)

MY LITTLE LOVE NEST WAS A TERRIBLE TRAP
WITH ME BEHAVING LIKE A SIMPERING SAP
AND SO I'M LOOKING FOR A SPOT ON THE MAP
IF HE'S GOIN' SOUTH, I'M GOIN' NORTH
IF HE'S GOIN' BACK, I'M GOIN' FORTH
(*stands*)
WHEREVER HE AIN'T!

(*makes grand exit,* S.R. *but pops on stage for button of song
    with "I'll show him" expression*)

(*J.G.#4 marches on* S.R. *as "pied piper" with the front section of
    a long holiday garland over her shoulder and with her head
    adorned with a Santa hat. She sings:*)

WE NEED A LITTLE CHRISTMAS (as a madrigal)

J.G.#4.
HAUL OUT THE HOLLY

(*Other girls enter on cue, all with the same long garland draped
    over their shoulders, and join in the merry carrolling.*)

J.G.#3.
PUT UP THE TREE BEFORE MY SPIRIT FALLS AGAIN
    J.G.#2.
FILL UP THE STOCKING

(*J.G.#1 follows with*)

J.G.#1.
I MAY BE RUSHING THINGS, BUT
    ALL.
DECK THE HALLS AGAIN, NOW
FOR WE NEED A LITTLE CHRISTMAS
RIGHT THIS VERY MINUTE,
CANDLES IN THE WINDOW
CAROLS AT THE SPINET
YES, WE NEED A LITTLE CHRISTMAS
RIGHT THIS VERY MINUTE

J.G.#4.
IT HASN'T SNOWED A SINGLE FLURRY
J.G.#1.
BUT SANTA, DEAR, WE'RE IN A HURRY
ALL.
SO, CLIMB DOWN THE CHIMNEY
TURN ON THE BRIGHTEST STRING OF LIGHTS I'VE
   EVER SEEN
SLICE UP THE FRUIT CAKE
IT'S TIME WE HUNG SOME TINSEL
ON THAT EVERGREEN BOW

FOR WE NEED A LITTLE MUSIC
NEED A LITTLE LAUGHTER,
NEED A LITTLE SINGING
RINGING THRU THE RAFTER
AND WE NEED A LITTLE SNAPPY
"HAPPY EVER AFTER"
NEED A LITTLE CHRISTMAS, NOW!

(*Musical dance interlude as girls wrap J.G.#1 in the garland
    and they skip joyfully to the music. After interlude, the
    girls pose around the "Human Christmas Tree' and sing:*)

J.G.#1.
FOR WE NEED A LITTLE MUSIC
(*Other girls sing "Fa-la-la's" in counter-harmony.*)
NEED A LITTLE LAUGHTER
NEED A LITTLE SINGING
RINGING THRU THE RAFTER
AND WE NEED A LITTLE SNAPPY
"HAPPY EVER AFTER"
NEED A LITTLE CHRISTMAS, NOW!

(*At the end of the song, the girls move forward on music cue
    and remove J.G.#1's Santa hat to reveal a bright silver star
    atop her head. During playoff, the girls dance about and
    place two director's chairs onstage. One (with the name
    MACK) is set U.R. preset with a fedora hat. The other (with
    the name MABEL) is set U.L. with a small rag doll on its
    seat. J.G.#3 removes her Santa hat and puts on the fedora
    from MACK's chair, stands and sings:*)

I WON'T SEND ROSES (with a flavor of masculinity)

J.G.#3.
I WON'T SEND ROSES
OR HOLD THE DOOR
I WON'T REMEMBER
WHICH DRESS YOU WORE.
MY HEART IS TOO MUCH IN CONTROL,
THE LACK OF ROMANCE IN MY SOUL
WILL TURN YA GRAY, KID
SO STAY AWAY, KID

FORGET MY SHOULDER
WHEN YOU'RE IN NEED
FORGETTING BIRTHDAYS
IS GUARANTEED.
AND SHOULD I LOVE YOU
YOU WOULD BE – THE LAST TO KNOW
I WON'T SEND ROSES
AND ROSES SUIT YOU – SO.
(*moves* C.)

MY PACE IS FRANTIC
MY TEMPER'S CROSS
WITH WORDS ROMANTIC
I'M AT A LOSS
I'D BE THE FIRST ONE TO AGREE
THAT I'M PREOCCUPIED WITH ME
AND IT'S INBRED KID
SO, KEEP YOUR HEAD, KID

IN ME YOU'LL FIND THINGS
LIKE GUTS AND NERVE
BUT NOT THE KIND THINGS
THAT YOU DESERVE
AND SO WHILE THERE'S A FIGHTING CHANCE
JUST TURN AND GO
I WON'T SEND ROSES
AND ROSES SUIT YOU – SO

(*Removes hat, crosses* S.L. *to "MABEL" chair, picks up rag doll,*

clutches it as she sits and sings softly with femininity and a
gentle resignation:)

SO WHO NEEDS ROSES
OR STUFF LIKE THAT
AND WHO NEEDS CHOCOLATES
THEY MAKE ME FAT
AND I CAN GET ALONG JUST FINE
WITHOUT A GUSHING VALENTINE
AND I'LL GET BY, KID
WITH JUST THE GUY, KID

AND IF HE CALLS ME
AND IT'S COLLECT
SIR WALTER RALEIGH
I DON'T EXPECT
AND THOUGH I KNOW I MAY BE LEFT
OUT ON A LIMB
SO WHO NEEDS ROSES
THAT DIDN'T COME FROM HIM

(*She hugs doll gently and looks toward "MACK'S" chair as a*
spot brightens on it and then fades. On applause J.G.#1
enters US.L., *stands looking at "Roses" soloist who is sitting*
quietly holding her doll, and then on music cue taps forward
to cheer-up J.G.#3. She sings a la Shirley Temple:)

TAP YOUR TROUBLES AWAY

J.G.#1.
TAP
(*taps foot and frightens J.G.#3*)
YOUR TROUBLES AWAY
YOU'VE BOUNCED A BIG CHECK
YOUR MOM HAS THE VAPORS

TAP
YOUR TROUBLES AWAY
YOUR CAR HAD A WRECK
THEY'RE SERVING YOU PAPERS
WHEN YOU'RE THE ONE THAT IT ALWAYS RAINS ON
SIMPLY TRY PUTTING YOUR MARY-JANES ON
(*reveals tap shoes for J.G.#3, who excitedly takes them and puts*
them on)

YOUR BOSS
JUST GAVE YOU THE AX
THERE'S YEARS OF BACK TAX
YOU SIMPLY CAN'T PAY

IF A SKY FULL OF CRAP
ALWAYS LANDS IN YOUR LAP
MAKE A CURTSY—AND
(*On this phrase, other girls enter to join in the singing and danc-
     ing.*)
TAP YOUR TROUBLES AWAY

(*A tap routine begins with all but J.G.#3, she observes the fun
     for a moment, and then on music cue squeals with joy and
     runs* DS. *to participate.*)

   ALL.
WHEN YOU NEED SOMETHING TO TURN YOUR MIND
     OFF
WHY NOT TRY TAPPING YOUR POOR BEHIND OFF

(*The dance number continues and builds to a feverish tempo and
     ends with showstopping panache. All exit but J.G.#4 who
     is handed straw boater and cane from* S.R., *puts on boater,
     leans forward on cane* C.)

   J.G.#4.
FOR I WAS BORN
TO PLAY THE TWO-A-DAY
THE HOKE, THE CORN,
THE EMPTY MATINEE

AND SO I KNOW
(*places cane on her shoulder and moves* DS.R.)
THAT VAUD'VILLE'S JUST ASLEEP
AND SO I GOTTA KEEP ON
DANCIN' TILL I RAKE IT UP
AND DIG IT UP AND WAKE IT UP!

I GET NO THRILL
(*strolls* S.L.)
FROM THIS ATOMIC AGE
MY HOME IS STILL

UPON THE PALACE STAGE
(*gestures with the cane*)

WHERE LIFE'S A SONG
AS I LONG AS I CAN SAY
I BELONG TO THE WONDERFUL
WORLD OF THE TWO-A-DAY!

(*On tempo change she moves* US.R. *and uses her cane to bring
J.G.#2 and #3 Center. Both are wearing decorated straw
boaters.*)

BOSOM BUDDIES

(*This number and the others in this medley are done in the
famous "Gallagher and Sheen" vaudeville style.*)

J.G.#2,3.
WE'LL ALWAYS BE BOSOM BUDDIES
FRIENDS, SISTERS AND PALS
WE'LL ALWAYS BE BOSOM BUDDIES
IF LIFE SHOULD REJECT YOU
THERE'S ME TO PROTECT YOU
J.G.#3.
IF I SAY THAT YOUR TONGUE IS VICIOUS
J.G.#2.
IF I CALL YOU UNCOUTH
IT'S SIMPLY THAT
WHO ELSE BUT A BOSOM BUDDY
WILL SIT DOWN AND TELL YOU THE TRUTH
J.G.#3.
I FEEL IT'S MY DUTY TO TELL YOU IT'S TIME TO
(*both moving* DS.C.)
ADJUST TO YOUR AGE
YOU TRY TO BE "PEG O' MY HEART"
WHEN YOU'RE "LADY MACBETH"
EXACTLY HOW OLD ARE YOU, VERA
THE TRUTH!
J.G.#2.
HOW OLD DO YOU THINK?
J.G.#3.
I'D SAY SOMEWHERE BETWEEN
40 AND DEATH

J.G.#2,3.
(*nose to nose*)
BUT SWEETIE
I'LL ALWAYS BE ALICE TOKLAS
IF YOU'LL BE GERTRUDE STEIN
    J.G.#2.
AND THO' I'LL ADMIT I'VE DISHED YOU
I'VE GOSSIPED AND GLOATED
BUT I'M SO DEVOTED.
    J.G.#3.
AND IF I SAY THAT SEX AND GUTS
MADE YOU INTO A STAR
IT'S SIMPLY THAT
    J.G.#2,3.
WHO ELSE BUT A BOSOM BUDDY
WILL TELL YOU HOW ROTTEN YOU ARE

WHO ELSE BUT A BOSOM BUDDY
(*very broad, a la Durante and Hope*)
WILL SIT DOWN AND LEVEL AND
GIVE YOU THE DEVIL AND
SIT DOWN AND TELL YOU THE TRUTH!

(*Big finish! They exit* S.L. *as J.G.#1 enters* S.R. *wearing a straw-boater topped with a rubber chicken and holding a "hammer-slammer" noisemaker that she uses during the number.*)

I WANNA MAKE THE WORLD LAUGH

(*a la Groucho Marx, the Three Stooges, and/or Eddie Cantor*)

    J.G.#1.
HEARTBREAK AND PASSION
MAY BOTH BE IN FASHION
BUT I WANNA MAKE THE WORLD LAUGH

LET OTHERS DO DRAMA
OF SIN AND DISGRACE
WHILE I THROW A FISH IN
THE HEROINE'S FACE!

TO KEEP THEM IN STITCHES

I'D BURN THE STAR'S BRITCHES
AND SAW COUSIN SALLY IN HALF
LET ALL THE OTHERS DEAL WITH HUMANITY'S WOES
I'D RATHER BE THE GUY WITH THE FLY ON HIS NOSE

MY GOAL AND MY MISSION
MY BURNING AMBITION IS
(*hits pianist on head with "hammer-slammer"*)
I WANNA MAKE THE WORLD
LAUGH!
(*into*)

THE MAN IN THE MOON

(*J.G.#2,3,4 enter* US.L. *and pose as a heavenly choir. J.G.#1 faces* U.S. *and conducts them with her "hammer-slammer" until she turns dramatically front to perform: a la Rudolph Frimel.*)

THE MAN IN THE MOON
IS A LADY   J.G.#1.
A LADY   AH, AH, AH, AH
WITH LIPSTICK AND   J.G.#1.
  CURLS   AH, AH, AH, AH
  (ALL.)
THE COW THAT JUMPED OVAH
CRIED, "JUMPIN' JEHOVAH
I THINK IT'S JUST ONE OF THE GIRLS"
(*All exit but J.G. #4, who gets cane from piano and sings: into*)

SO LONG, DEARIE

  J.G.#4.
WAVE YOUR LITTLE HAND AND WHISPER "SO LONG,
  DEARIE"
YOU AIN'T GONNA SEE ME ANY MORE
BUT WHEN YOU DISCOVER THAT YOUR LIFE IS DREARY
DON'T YOU COME A KNOCKIN' AT MY DOOR

FOR I'LL BE ALL DOLLED UP
(*struts* DS.R.)
AND SINGING THAT SONG

THAT SAYS "YOU DOG
I TOLD YOU SO"

SO WAVE YOUR LITTLE HAND AND WHISPER, "SO
    LONG, DEARIE,"
DEARIE SHOULD HAVE SAID, "SO LONG," SO LONG
    AGO
(*moves* s.l.)
BECAUSE YOU TREATED ME SO ROTTEN AND ROUGH
I'VE HAD ENOUGH OF FEELING LOW
SO WAVE YOUR LITTLE HAND AND WHISPER "SO
    LONG, DEARIE,"
DEARIE SHOULD HAVE SAID, "SO LONG," SO LONG
    AGO

(*J.G.#1 and #3 enter and sing with J.G.#4.*)

I GET NO THRILL FROM THIS ATOMIC AGE
MY HOME IS STILL UPON THE PALACE STAGE
WHERE LIFE'S A SONG — AS LONG AS I CAN SAY
I BELONG TO THE WONDERFUL WORLD OF THE
TWO-A-DAY!
(*Trio moves* ds.c.)
    J.G.#1.
WHERE I CAN TELL MY JOKES
    J.G.#3.
SING MY SONG
    J.G.#4.
SHOW THE FOLKS THAT I BELONG
    ALL.
TO THE WONDERFUL WORLD OF THE TWO-A-DAY!
(*dance tag and bows*)

(*J.G.#2 enters wearing a boa. She glances around the stage for a
    moment, then sits atop the piano and sings:*)

IF HE WALKED INTO MY LIFE

(*combining the honest acting of the lyric with the style of a
    torch song*)

J.G.#2.
WHERE'S THAT BOY WITH THE BUGLE?
MY LITTLE LOVE
WHO WAS ALWAYS MY BIG ROMANCE
WHERE'S THAT BOY WITH THE BUGLE?
AND WHY DID I EVER BUY HIM THOSE DAMN LONG
   PANTS?

DID HE NEED A STRONGER HAND?
DID HE NEED A LIGHTER TOUCH?
WAS I SOFT OR WAS I TOUGH?
DID I GIVE ENOUGH?
DID I GIVE TOO MUCH?

AT THE MOMENT THAT HE NEEDED ME,
DID I EVER TURN AWAY?
WOULD I BE THERE WHEN HE CALLED
IF HE WALKED INTO MY LIFE TODAY?

WERE HIS DAYS A LITTLE DULL?
WERE HIS NIGHTS A LITTLE WILD?
DID I OVERSTATE MY PLAN?
DID I STRESS THE MAN
AND FORGET THE CHILD?

AND THERE MUST HAVE BEEN A MILLION THINGS
THAT MY HEART FORGOT TO SAY
WOULD I THINK OF ONE OR TWO
IF HE WALKED INTO MY LIFE TODAY?

SHOULD I BLAME THE TIMES I PAMPERED HIM
OR BLAME THE TIMES I BOSSED HIM
WHAT A SHAME
I NEVER REALLY FOUND THE BOY
BEFORE I LOST HIM.

(*gets off piano*)
WERE THE YEARS A LITTLE FAST?
WAS HIS WORLD A LITTLE FREE?
WAS THERE TOO MUCH OF A CROWD
ALL TOO LUSH AND LOUD
AND NOT ENOUGH OF ME?

THOUGH I'LL ASK MYSELF MY WHOLE LIFE LONG,
WHAT WENT WRONG ALONG THE WAY

WOULD I MAKE THE SAME MISTAKES
IF HE WALKED INTO MY LIFE TODAY?
IF THAT BOY WITH THE BUGLE
WALKED INTO MY LIFE TODAY.

(*J.G.#2 exits. Other girls enter on music wearing red feather "Dolly" headpieces. They also carry life-size cutouts of Jerry Herman dressed as a waiter that they reveal on cue. What follows is a light-hearted spoof of Jerry's famous title song:*)

HELLO, DOLLY!

(*as Carol Channing*)
   J.G.#3.
HELLO, JERRY!
WELL, HELLO, LOUIE!

(*As Pearl Bailey, J.G.#4 talks:*)

   J.G.#4.
WELL, HONEY, I GUESS I DON'T HAVE TO TELL
YA THAT PEARLIE MAE IS SO GLAD TO BE BACK
BUT MY FEET ARE KILLING ME, HONEY!

(*As Barbra Streisand, J.G.#2 sings:*)

   J.G.#2.
YOU'RE LOOKING SWELL, GORGEOUS
I CAN TELL, GORGEOUS

(*As Ethel Merman, J.G.#1 sings:*)

   J.G.#1.
YOU'RE STILL GLOWIN'
YOU'RE STILL CROWIN'
YOU'RE STILL GOIN' STRONG

(*All move* DS. *and line up beside their cut-out. As they do the foreign language section, they relate appropriately to the cardboard Jerry. J.G.#4, does Geisha Girl bow and sings Oriental style:*)

    J.G.#4.
AH-SO
DORI . . . HA! (*ends with a karate chop*) (*like an Italian opera, to the tune of Un Bel Di*)
    J.G.#3.
OH, BON BIORNO
DOLLY . . .

(*in a French style a la Edith Piaf*)

    J.G.#1.
IL EST UNE DE VOS CHANSON LA PLUS FAMUSE . . .

(*in a 'Gestapo' style*)

    J.G.#2.
ACTUNG, DOLLY!
DIE LIEST BEIR SWEINHART, DOLLY!

(*As music continues all Girls ad lib their 'language' for a few moments. Then as music changes they move U.S. with the cut-outs and line them facing R. as they speak.*)

    J.G.#3.
JERRY'S LITTLE ANTHEM HAS SOLD TICKETS
    J.G.#4.
RECORDS
    J.G.#1.
PRESIDENTS
    J.G.#2.
(*as a television spokeswoman*)
AND HAMBURGERS! WHENEVER
MY DARLING STANLEY IS OUT OF TOWN, I TAKE ALL OF OUR
KIDS AND WE HURRY ON DOWN TO HARDEES! BECAUSE OF THAT
WONDERFUL HAMBURGER SONG WE ALL HEARD ON T.V. AH, LET'S SING IT FOR THEM KIDS:

ALL.
(*as hungry kids*)
HELLO, HARDEE'S!
WELL, HELLO HARDEE'S
FOR THAT CHARBROILED TASTE
WE LOVE FROM WAY BACK WHEN
SO, GOODBYE FRIED IN OIL BURGERS
HERE EAT THE REAL CHARBROILED BURGERS
HARDEE'S THE TASTE THAT BRINGS US BACK AGAIN.

(*Girls place cutouts in a semi-circle, facing* US., *stand on* US.L.
*level and wave to the "delegates at the convention." J.G.#3,
as Lady Bird, speaks in an exaggerated okie accent:*)

J.G.#3.
LYNDON AND I AND ALL THE BYRDS. LUCY BAINES . . .
J.G.#1.
HI
(*She waves.*)
J.G.#3.
LYNDA BIRD
(*J.G.#2 curtseys.*)
AND
(*turns to black cast member who gives her a strong look in
return*)
OH . . .
EVERYBODY ARE HAPPY TO BE HERE AT THE DEMO-
CRATIC
NATIONAL CONVENTION. AND WE ARE SO VERY
THRILLED THAT
JERRY HERMAN HAS GIVEN US HIS FINE BROADWAY
TUNE TO
HELP GET LYNDON ELECTED. WOULD YOU LIKE TO
HEAR THAT
SONG NOW? WELL NOW OF COURSE YOU WOULD!
(*with a drawl please*)
ALL.
HELLO, LYNDON!
WELL, HELLO, LYNDON!
WE'RE SO PROUD THAT YOU'RE THE MAN
THE COUNTRY CHEERS.
(*All wave.*)

J.G.#3.
BE OUR GUIDE, LYNDON!
(*hands over hearts*)
LADY BIRD AT YOUR SIDE, LYNDON!
ALL.
PROMISE YOU'LL STAY WITH US FOR
FOUR MORE YEARS!
(*Women perform choreographed dance with the cut-outs.*)
J.G.#1.
PLEASE!
J.G.#2.
SING!
J.G.#3.
ALONG!
J.G.#4.
WITH US!

(*House lights up to half as girls lead the audience in the sing-a-long.*)

ALL.
I FEEL THE ROOM SWAYIN'
FOR THE BAND'S PLAYIN'
ONE OF MY OLD FAV'RITE SONGS
FROM WAY BACK WHEN
SO . . . GOLLY GEE, FELLOWS!
FIND HER A VACANT KNEE, FELLOWS!
DOLLY, YOU'LL NEVER GO AWAY!
DOLLY, YOU'LL NEVER GO AWAY!
DOLLY, YOU'LL NEVER GO AWAY AGAIN!
(*All salute. American flag unfurls on final chord of music.*)

END OF PART ONE

PART TWO

A "Movie Medley" begins Part Two. J.G.#1 and 4 enter U.R. *and the other two girls enter* U.L. *They wear black character hats (Chaplin, cowboy, gangster, flapper) and a single black accessory (bow tie, western string tie, four-in-hand tie, scarf). After fanfare, they sing the first song brightly and simply, without over-characterizing each star reference:*

JUST GO TO THE MOVIES

J.G.#1,4.
SO IF PURE ENTERTAINMENT'S YOUR STYLE
    J.G.#2,3.
FOLLOW ME, I HAVE TWO ON THE AISLE
    J.G.#4.
NEED TO RELAX?
NEED TO ESCAPE?
GO SEE FAY WRAY IN THE PALM OF AN APE
WATCH ERROL FLYNN SHOOTING HIS BOW
(*indicates a bow*)
    ALL.
JUST GO TO THE MOVIES
JUST GO TO A PICTURE SHOW, OH
    J.G.#1.
WHEN YOUR MORALE
NEEDS SOME REPAIRS
WATCH BUSBY'S BEAUTIES DESCENDING THE STAIRS
(*J.G.#1,4 move* DS. *imitating movie beauty.*)
HUNDREDS OF GIRLS DOIN' HIGH KICKS
(*Both do kicks.*)
    ALL.
JUST GO TO THE MOVIES
JUST GO TO THE FLICKS
    J.G.#2.
AND ALL FOR THE SUM
OF A QUARTER, LIFE IS PEACHY
YOU CAN BECOME
ALICE FAYE OR DON AMECHE

J.G.#3.
SWAMPED WITH YOUR BILLS?
LATE WITH YOUR RENT?
WATCH BETTE DAVIS RUN OUT ON GEORGE BRENT
(*does Davis hand gesture*)
SEE FRED ASTAIRE
STEPPIN' IN STYLE
(*imitates Astaire dance step*)
    ALL.
WHEN EVERYTHING'S DARK AND UPSET
GO CALLING ON CLARK AND CLAUDETTE.
(*famous hitchiking pose from "It Happened One Night"*)
JUST GO TO A MARVELOUS MOVIE
AND SMILE.
(*All girls move* DS.C., *face* US. *in straight line. When they sing, they face front; otherwise they have their backs to the audience.*)
    J.G.#2.
GIRLS IN SARONGS
MONSTERS IN CAPES
SEE SCARLET MAKE A DRESS OUT OF THE DRAPES
    J.G.#1.
LIFE CAN BE GRAND
FROM THE THIRD ROW
    ALL.
JUST GO TO THE MOVIES
JUST GO TO A PICTURE SHOW, OH
    J.G.#4.
COOPER IN "WINGS"
    J.G.#3.
CRAWFORD IN "RAIN"
    J.G.#1.
WATCH TARZAN BEAT HIS CHEST WHEN HE MEETS
    JANE
    J.G.#4.
SING WITH DICK POWELL
    J.G.#2.
RIDE WITH TOM MIX
    ALL.
JUST GO TO THE MOVIES
JUST GO TO THE FLICKS
VICARIOUSLY

(*moving* DS.C.)
YOU ARE FLYING DOWN TO RIO
(*lean in for movie closeup*)
SHARE THE MARQUEE
WITH MISSUS MARX'S ZANY TRIO.
(*Marx Brothers imitations*)

SO WHEN YOUR LIFE
(*J.G.#1 moves* U.L.)
SEEMS A BIT LEAN
(*J.G.#2 moves* U.L.)
JUST LET SOME SHADOWS APPEAR ON THE SCREEN,
(*J.G.#3 moves* U.L.)
SHINE LIKE A STAR
(*J.G.#4 moves* U.L.)
FOR A BRIEF WHILE

WHENEVER YOU'RE DOWN IN THE DUMPS
TRY PUTTING ON JUDY'S RED PUMPS
(*click heels, cross fingers*)
JUST GO TO A MARVELOUS MOVIE
AND SMILE!

(*Stage lights flicker like a movieola. Melodramatic villain music begins, J.G.#4 does a villainous laugh. Other girls scream as J.G.#4 chases them offstage. When she reaches* U.R., *she laughs and sings:*)

MOVIES WERE MOVIES

J.G.#4.
MOVIES WERE MOVIES
WHEN YOU PAID A DIME TO ESCAPE
(*runs* DS.L.)
CHEERING THE HERO AND
HISSING THE MAN IN THE CAPE
(*strikes villain pose*)
ROMANCE AND ACTION AND THRILLS
(*prospector pose*)
PARTNER, THAR'S GOLD IN THEM HILLS
MOVIES WERE MOVIES
WHEN DURING THE TITLES YOU'D KNOW
YOU'D GET A HAPPY ENDING

DOZENS OF BLUNDERING COPS
IN A THUNDERING CHASE
(*runs in place a la Keystone Cop*)
GETTING A BANG OUT OF LEMON MERINGUE
(*ducks to miss pie*)
IN THE FACE

BANDITS ATTACKING A TRAIN
(*gallops in place*)
ONE LITTLE TRAMP WITH A CANE
(*Charlie Chaplin walk*)
MOVIES WERE MOVIES
WERE MOVIES
WHEN I RAN THE SHOW

(*More melodramatic villain music. Lights flicker. J.G.#1 enters, sees J.G.#4, screams and is chased around the stage for a moment. A percussion gunshot is heard. Villain exits. A frightened J.G.#1 cowers* US., *back to audience. She turns slowly and sings:*)

LOOK WHAT HAPPENED TO MABEL

(*The number begins ad-lib, quietly and mounts in rhythm and excitement. J.G.#1 sees her image on the screen for the first time and is in awe.*)

J.G.#1.
SEE THAT FASCINATING CREATURE
WITH PERFECTION STAMPED ON EVERY FEATURE
SHE WAS PLAIN LITTLE NELLIE
THE KID FROM THE DELI
BUT MOTHER OF GOD
LOOK WHAT HAPPENED TO MABEL!

FROM NOW ON THIS PILE OF FLESH'LL
BE CONSIDERED SOMETHIN' PRETTY SPECIAL
AND MISS B.L.T. DOWN
IS THE TOAST OF THE TOWN
MARY AND JOSEPH
WHAT HAPPENED TO MABEL!
(*becoming more confident*)
EVERY GESTURE AND POSITION

THAT SHE TAKES
IS SMART AND METICULOUS
TALK ABOUT THE MAGIC
THAT A CAMERA MAKES
BUT THIS IS RIDICULOUS!

HOLD YOUR TONGUE
AND HOLD YOUR SNICKERS
FOR THE NEW ENCHANTRESS
OF THE FLICKERS
IS THAT PLAIN LITTLE NELLIE
THE KID FROM THE DELI
SO RATTLE-ME-BEADS
LOOK WHAT HAPPENED TO MABEL!

(*with a stripper-like strut*)
I KNOW THAT YOU MIGHT THINK I'M BALMY
BUT THE QUEEN OF CORNED BEEF AND SALAMI
IS A GLAMOROUS GODDESS
WHO'S BUSTIN' HER BODICE
(*shakes her bosom*)
OH! JUMPING SAINT JUDE
LOOK WHAT HAPPENED TO MABEL!

(*Number ends like it started, with J.G.#1 facing* us. *in stylish pose.*)

NELSON

(*On musical introduction, J.G.#1 exits as J.G.#3 enters* u.r., *does an operetta dance turn, and sings a la Jeanette Mac-Donald:*)

J.G.#3.
MY HEART, MY LOVE
MY LIFE IS HIS ALONE
BUT IF
BUT IF
BUT IF THE TRUTH BE KNOWN

MY HERO MUST STAND
ON A BOX IN OUR LOVE SCENES
AND, GOD, DOES HE ACT LIKE A LOX

IN OUR LOVE SCENES
OH, NELSON
WHAT YOU'RE PUTTING ME THROUGH, OO OO OO OO.
(*hand cupped at her mouth*)

ALL OF HIS NOTES ABOVE B FLAT -VERBOTTEN
AND ALL OF HIS NOTES BELOW B FLAT ARE ROTTEN
OH, NELSON
DON'T CALL ME, I'LL CALL YOU, OO OO OO OO

HIS LOVEMAKING CASTS SUCH A PALL
IT'S HARD NOT TO SLEEP THRU IT ALL
HIS VOCAL CHORDS CARRY
INSURANCE BY LLOYDS
AND SO, MIGHT I ADD
SHOULD HIS ADENOIDS.

THE LIGHTS WILT HIS HAIRDO
ON CAMERA HE'LL PRIMP
AND QUITE FRANKLY, HIS HAIR
ISN'T ALL THAT GOES LIMP
DARLING NELSON
HOW INCREDIBLY BORING
THAT'S NOT SINGING, THAT'S SNORING!
WHAT YOU'RE PUTTING ME THROUGH!

THE PICTURE OF STRENGTH
AND GOOD BREEDING, OF COURSE
AND OF PASSION AND WARMTH
(I'M DISCUSSING HIS HORSE)
DARLING NELSON
DON'T CALL ME, I'LL CALL YOU, OO OO OO OO.

A SYMBOL OF VIRTUE AND CLASS
AMERICA'S SWEETHEARTS MY ASS
A PAIR MADE IN HEAVEN
THE FANS LOVE TO SAY
BUT EACH TIME WE KISS
I'D SWEAR THAT HE'S GAY
(*swaying*)
IN FILM AFTER FILM
AFTER FILM I BETROTHED HIM

WE SNUGGLED AND SMOOCHED
AND OH GOD, HOW I LOATHED HIM
MY, NELSON
OH SO CALMING
YOU'LL NEVER NEED EMBALMING
OH NELSON
WHAT YOU'RE PUTTING ME THROUGH
(*big operetta finish*)

(*J.G.#1, #2, #4 join #3 on* U.R. *platforms for a reprise of*)

JUST GO TO THE MOVIES

ALL.
SO WHEN YOUR LIFE
SEEMS A BIT LEAN
JUST LET SOME SHADOWS
APPEAR ON THE SCREEN
SHINE LIKE A STAR
FOR A BRIEF WHILE
WHENEVER YOU'RE DOWN IN THE DUMPS
TRY PUTTING ON JUDY'S RED PUMPS
(*Click heels, cross fingers. All move* L. *on their solo lines.*)
J.G.#3.
AND VISIT A GUN TOTIN' SHARPIE
J.G.#4.
A MOTH-EATEN HARPIE
J.G.#2.
A DANGEROUS BEAUTY
J.G.#1.
A KEWPIE DOLL CUTIE
ALL.
AN ANCIENT HIGH LAMA
A HIGH STEPPIN' MAMA
(*All move* D.C.)
JUST GO TO THE MOVIES AND
SMILE!

(*On final bars of music, girls do peek-a-boo poses. During
playoff music, they do fast bows and exit. J.G.#2 removes
her hat and tie, gives it to J.G.#4, moves* R. *and sings
warmly:*)

SHALOM

J.G.#2.
SHALOM, SHALOM
YOU'LL FIND SHALOM
THE NICEST GREETING YOU KNOW
IT MEANS BONJOUR, SALUD
AND SKOAL
AND TWICE AS MUCH AS HELLO
(*moves* C.)
IT MEANS A MILLION LOVELY THINGS
LIKE PEACE BE YOURS, WELCOME HOME
AND EVEN WHEN YOU SAY GOODBYE
IF YOUR VOICE HAS "I DON'T WANT TO GO" IN IT
SAY GOODBYE WITH A LITTLE "HELLO" IN IT
AND SAY GOODBYE WITH
ALL.
SHALOM
(*J.G.#2 joins other girls who enter and stand on* U.L. *platform
    levels.*)
SHALOM
SHALOM

MILK AND HONEY
(*sung as an optimistic anthem*)

ALL.
THIS IS THE LAND OF MILK AND HONEY
THIS IS THE LAND OF SUN AND SONG AND
THIS IS THE WORLD OF GOOD AND PLENTY
HUMBLE AND PROUD
AND YOUNG AND STRONG

AND THIS IS THE PLACE
WHERE THE HOPES OF THE HOMELESS
AND THE DREAMS
OF THE LOST COMBINE
THIS IS THE LAND THAT HEAVEN BLESSED
AND THIS LOVELY LAND IS MINE
J.G.#2.
WHAT IF THE EARTH IS DRY AND BARREN
WHAT IF THE MORNING SUN IS MEAN TO US

FOR THIS IS A STATE OF MIND WE LIVE IN
WE WANT IT GREEN AND
   ALL.
SO IT'S GREEN TO US
FOR WHEN YOU HAVE
WONDERFUL PLANS FOR TOMORROW
SOMEHOW EVEN TODAY LOOKS FINE
SO, WHAT IF IT'S ROCK AND DUST AND SAND
THIS LOVELY LAND IS MINE
THIS LOVELY LAND IS MINE
THIS LOVELY LAND IS MINE

(*All girls exit except J.G.#1, who crosses stage to* U.R. *platform, turns slowly forward and sings quietly:*)

TIME HEALS EVERYTHING

   J.G.#1.
TIME HEALS EVERYTHING
TUESDAY, THURSDAY
TIME HEALS EVERYTHING
APRIL, AUGUST
IF I'M PATIENT, THE BREAK WILL MEND
AND SOME FINE MORNING THE HURT WILL END

SO MAKE THE MOMENTS FLY
AUTUMN, WINTER
I'LL FORGET YOU BY
NEXT YEAR, SOME YEAR
THOUGH IT'S HELL THAT I'M GOING THROUGH
SOME TUESDAY, THURSDAY, APRIL, AUGUST
AUTUMN, WINTER, NEXT YEAR, SOME YEAR
TIME HEALS EVERYTHING, TIME HEALS EVERYTHING
BUT LOVING YOU

IF I'M PATIENT THE BREAK WILL MEND
AND SOME FINE MORNING THE HURT WILL END
(*During music interlude she crosses* C. *to piano and continues
   with bravado:*)
SO MAKE THE MOMENTS FLY
AUTUMN, WINTER
I'LL FORGET YOU BY

NEXT YEAR, SOME YEAR
THOUGH IT'S HELL THAT I'M GOING THROUGH
SOME TUESDAY, THURSDAY, APRIL, AUGUST
AUTUMN, WINTER, NEXT YEAR, SOME YEAR
TIMES HEALS EVERYTHING, TIME HEALS EVERYTHING
BUT LOVING YOU

(*"It's Today" Dance Section follows, as J.G.#1 sits atop the grand piano, puts on her feathered turban that matches the other dancing girls'. They all carry champagne glasses that are used throughout the next number.*)

MAME

(*The fun of this number is playing against the song's usual full-throttle style. It is sung in an almost staccato whisper with deadpan sophistication. Verse by verse the number gets quieter, until the final "Mame" is only mouthed.*)

ALL.
YOU COAX THE BLUES RIGHT OUT OF THE HORN
MAME
(*All lean.*)
YOU CHARM THE HUSKS RIGHT OFF OF THE CORN
MAME
(*champagne toast*)
YOU'VE GOT THE BANJOS STRUMMIN'
(*Girls move* DS. *as "one."*)
AND PLUCKIN' OUT A TUNE TO BEAT THE BAND
THE WHOLE PLANTATION'S HUMMIN'
SINCE YOU BROUGHT DIXIE
BACK TO DIXIELAND
(*All move* S.R.)
YOU MAKE THE COTTON EASY TO PICK
MAME,
(*lean*)
YOU GIVE MY OLE MINT JULIP A KICK
MAME,
(*toast*)
YOU MAKE THE OLD MAGNOLIA TREE
BLOSSOM AT THE MENTION OF YOUR NAME

(*Girls move to various areas of stage and pose.*)
YOU'VE MADE US FEEL ALIVE AGAIN
YOU'VE GIVEN US THE DRIVE AGAIN
TO MAKE THE SOUTH REVIVE AGAIN
MAME

(*Still posed and without blinking an eye they sing.*)
YOU MAKE OUR BLACK-EYED PEAS AND OUR GRITS
MAME
SEEM LIKE THE BILL OF FARE AT THE RITZ
MAME
YOU CAME, YOU SAW, YOU CONQUERED
AND ABSOLUTELY NOTHING IS THE SAME

YOUR SPECIAL FASCINATION'LL
PROVE TO BE INSPIRATIONAL
WE THINK YOU'RE JUST SENSATIONAL

(*Mame (only the lips move) on final chord of music girls offer a final toast. J.G.#1 and #3 exit, J.G.#2 and #4 remove turbans and move to* U.L. *levels, one standing profile, one front to sing this countermelody duet. It begins as a haunting echo and ends as a powerful duet.*)

KISS HER NOW

J.G.#4.
BEFORE YOU HALF REMEMBER
WHAT HER SMILE WAS LIKE
BEFORE YOU HALF RECALL
THE DAY YOU FOUND HER

KISS HER NOW
WHILE SHE'S YOUNG
KISS HER NOW
WHILE SHE'S YOURS
KISS HER NOW
WHILE SHE NEEDS YOUR ARMS AROUND HER
(*J.G.#2 joins*)
FOR IF YOU LET A MOMENT COME
BETWEEN YOU NOW

IT SOON BECOMES A DAY, A YEAR
A LIFETIME

BLINK YOUR EYE, TURN YOUR HEAD
AND YOU'VE LOST HER
AND YOU'LL SPEND HALF YOUR LIFE
WOND'RING HOW

SO BEFORE YOU FORGET
HOW YOU LOVED HER
KISS HER NOW
KISS HER NOW

FOR IF YOU LET A MOMENT
COME BETWEEN YOU NOW
IT SOON BECOMES A DAY, A YEAR
A LIFETIME

BLINK YOUR EYE, TURN YOUR HEAD
AND YOU'VE LOST HER
AND YOU'LL SPEND HALF YOUR LIFE
WONDERING HOW

SO BEFORE YOU FORGET
HOW YOU LOVED HER
KISS HER NOW
KISS HER NOW
KISS HER NOW
(*both turn slowly to face* US.)

THE TEA PARTY

(*Performed with a continental flavor. During "Dear World" interlude music, J.G.#1 and 3 enter* R. *wearing hats, gloves, shawls and pearls. They chatter and laugh as they cross* S.L. *and sit on levels. J.G.#2 enters* U.L. *with a tray of tea cups. She rattles the cups to stop the chatter, serves the tea, and speaks:*)

   J.G.#2.
I HAVEN'T BROUGHT YOU HERE JUST FOR A TEA
PARTY. I WANT TO DISCUSS THE PAST.

    J.G.#1.
THE PAST. WHAT MEMORIES I HAVE!
    J.G.#3.
GABRIELLE! TODAY WE NEED FACTS. NOT YOUR
    MADE
UP MEMORIES.
    J.G.#1.
HOW DARE YOU INSULT MY MEMORIES. THE NEXT
    THING
YOU'LL SAY IS THAT MY LITTLE DOG DICKIE DOESN'T
EXIST!

DICKIE

(*sung motherly as she strokes her dog*)

    J.G.#1.
DICKIE
DARLING LITTLE DICKIE
I'M SO PROUD OF MY LITTLE, PLUMP
LITTLE, SHY, LITTLE, CUDDLY CHAP

DICKIE
(*makes kissing sounds*)
DICKIE
ALWAYS LYING FLAT ON YOUR FAT TUMMY
HERE ON YOUR DEAR MUMMY'S LAP
STOP BARKING!
(*tenderly shakes her finger at "him"*)
EVEN
WHEN I HAVE TO SCOLD YOU
MUMMY'S JUST AS THRILLED AS CAN BE
HOW MAGNIFICENTLY YOU OBEY
    J.G.#3.
HE'S INCREDIBLY SPOILED!
    J.G.#1.
I WILL NOT SIT BACK AND
ALLOW YOU TO INSULT HIM THIS WAY

DICKIE, POOR DICKIE, DEAR DICKIE

THE FACT IS, MY DEARS, THAT
I DIDN'T EVEN BRING HIM TODAY!
   J.G.#2.
THERE! WE MUST HAVE AN EXPERT OPINION FROM AN
EXPERT AS TO WHETHER DICKIE EXISTS OR NOT.
(*takes drink of tea*)
   J.G.#3.
THEN I SHALL GO STRAIGHT HOME AND CONSULT MY VOICES:
(*standing and moving* D.L.)

VOICES (with hauteur)

CHATTER, CHATTER, CHATTER
THERE ARE VOICES IN YOUR PANTRY
THAT ARE WISHING YOU A HEARTY APPETITE!

GURGLE, GURGLE, GURGLE
THERE ARE VOICES IN YOUR TEA POT
(*peering into tea cup*)
WITH ADVICE FOR HOUSEWIVES

CHATTER, CHATTER, CHATTER
THERE ARE VOICES IN YOUR PILLOW
THAT HAVE COME TO TUCK YOU IN
AND SPEND THE NIGHT

AND VOICES IN YOUR VACUUM CLEANER
THAT CAN BE EXTREMELY IMPOLITE

CHATTER, CHATTER, CHATTER
THERE ARE VOICES IN YOUR CLOSET
SAYING "WEAR THE FUCHSIA GLOVES AND PURPLE
   VEIL!"
AND VOICES IN YOUR PIANO
SINGING UP AND DOWN THE ORIENTAL SCALE
(*turns to other girls*)

IF YOU WELCOME THEM AND TAKE THEM TO YOUR
   BOSOM

IT'S QUITE OBVIOUS INDEED
THAT THOSE LOVELY LITTLE VOICES ARE THE ONLY
  FRIENDS
A GIRL WILL EVER NEED

(*J.G.#2 stands and moves* R. *to piano as she speaks:*)

  J.G.#2.
I DON'T HEAR VOICES. OF COURSE WE COULD CON-
SULT VOLTAIRE.
  J.G.#1.
IS HE HERE?
  J.G.#3.
HE'S PLAYING WITH DICKIE, I SUPPOSE.
(returning to seat)
  J.G.#2.
OF COURSE. ALONG WITH OTHER GREAT MINDS OF
  THE
PAST OFFERING US THEIR HELP AND ADVICE!

THOUGHTS (with great assurance)

EVERYTHING THAT WAS, IS
EVERYTHING THAT LIVED, LIVES
EVERY LITTLE THOUGHT EVER THOUGHT
IS AS LASTING AS TIME.

EVERYTHING THAT WAS, IS
EVERYTHING THAT IS, WILL BE
SOME DISTANT DAY THEY'LL BE SAYING
THE SAYINGS THAT I'M—SAYING NOW

FOR, WE ARE NOT ALONE HERE
(looking around the "room")
THERE ARE OTHER MINDS HERE
MOLIERE AND KEATS ARE
ENRAGED AND ENGAGED IN A ROW
LISTEN TO THE LOVELY LANGUAGE
(directed to her guests)

ALL THE LESSONS VOLTAIRE EVER TAUGHT

AND ALL THE THOUGHTS THAT BUDDHA EVER
  THOUGHT
ARE RIGHT HERE, IN THIS AIR
IN THIS HOUSE, IN THIS ROOM
WITH US NOW!

(*All girls move* DS.C. *as music double-times and they sing in triple counterpoint. On the tag of the song, the trio does a grand opera bow. J.G.#1 and 2 exit* U.R. *as J.G.#3 crosses* D.R. *and sings with "a half-remembered smile":*)

AND I WAS BEAUTIFUL

   J.G.#3.
HE STOOD AND LOOKED AT ME
AND I WAS BEAUTIFUL
FOR IT WAS BEAUTIFUL
HOW HE BELIEVED IN ME

HIS LOVE WAS STRONG ENOUGH
TO MAKE ME ANYTHING
SO I WAS EVERYTHING
HE WANTED ME TO BE

BUT THEN HE WALKED AWAY
AND TOOK MY SMILE WITH HIM
AND NOW THE YEARS BLUR BY
BUT EVERY NOW AND THEN

I STOP AND THINK OF HIM
AND HOW HE LOOKED AT ME
AND ALL AT ONCE
I'M BEAUTIFUL, AGAIN
(*During music interlude she stands motionless* D.S.)
HIS LOVE WAS STRONG ENOUGH
TO MAKE ME ANYTHING
SO I WAS EVERYTHING
HE WANTED ME TO BE

BUT THEN HE WALKED AWAY
AND TOOK MY SMILE WITH HIM

AND NOW THE YEARS BLUR BY
BUT EVERY NOW AND THEN

I STOP AND THINK OF HIM
AND HOW HE LOOKED AT ME
AND ALL AT ONCE
I'M BEAUTIFUL AGAIN

FOR A MOMENT
I'M BEAUTIFUL AGAIN
(*As she smiles "softly", she touches her face with her gloved
    hands.*)

(*J.G.#3 exits* R. *as J.G.#1 lumbers up the* S.R. *ramp. She is
    obviously pregnant and slightly bewildered:*)

GOOCH'S SONG

    J.G.#1.
WITH MY WINGS RESOLUTELY SPREAD
MISSIS BURNSIDE
AND MY OLD INHIBITIONS SHED
MISSIS BURNSIDE
I DID EACH LITTLE THING YOU SAID
MISSIS BURNSIDE
I LIVED! I LIVED! I LIVED!

(*moving cautiously off platform*)
I ALTERED THE DRAPE OF
A DROP OF MY BODICE
AND SOFTENED THE SHAPE OF MY BROW
I FOLLOWED DIRECTIONS
AND MADE SOME CONNECTIONS
BUT WHAT DO I DO NOW?

(*Uses piano for support as she moves* U.C.)
WHO'D THINK THIS MISS PRIM WOULD
HAVE OPENED A WINDOW
AS FAR AS HER WHIM WOULD ALLOW
AND WHO WOULD SUPPOSE IT
WAS SO HARD TO CLOSE IT
OH, WHAT DO I DO NOW?

I POLISHED AND POWDERED
AND PUFFED MYSELF
IF LIFE IS A BANQUET
I STUFFED MYSELF

I HAD MY MISGIVINGS
BUT WENT ON A FIELD TRIP
TO FIND OUT WHAT LIVING'S ABOUT
MY THANKS FOR THE TRAINING
NOW I'M NOT COMPLAINING
BUT YOU LEFT SOMETHING OUT

AND SO I WANDERED OFF
AND I FOUND MY PRINCE
AND HAVE I BEEN NAUSEOUS
EVER SINCE
OH WHAT DO I DO NOW?

(*As orchestra plays "Dancing", J.G.#1 waltzes off* s.r. *as J.G.#2
    enters, observes the waltzing Gooch, then sings with a steady
    build.*)

BEFORE THE PARADE PASSES BY

J.G.#2.
BEFORE THE PARADE PASSES BY
I'M GONNA GO AND TASTE SATURDAY'S HIGHLIFE
BEFORE THE PARADE PASSES BY
I WANT TO GET SOME LIFE
BACK INTO MY LIFE

I'M READY TO MOVE OUT IN FRONT
I'VE HAD ENOUGH OF JUST PASSING BY LIFE
WITH THE REST OF THEM
WITH THE BEST OF THEM
I CAN HOLD MY HEAD UP HIGH

FOR I'VE GOT A GOAL AGAIN
I'VE GOTTA DRIVE AGAIN
I'M GONNA FEEL MY HEART COMING ALIVE AGAIN
BEFORE THE PARADE PASSES BY

(*crossing* DS.R.)
LOOK AT THAT CROWD UP AHEAD
LISTEN AND HEAR THAT BRASS HARMONY GLOWING
LOOK AT THAT CROWD UP AHEAD
PARDON ME IF MY OLD SPIRIT IS SHOWING (*moves* L.)
ALL OF THOSE LIGHTS OVER THERE
SEEM TO BE TELLING ME WHERE I'M GOING

WHEN THE WHISTLES BLOW
AND THE CYMBALS CRASH
AND THE SPARKLERS LIGHT THE SKY

I'M GONNA RAISE THE ROOF
I'M GONNA CARRY ON
GIVE ME AN OLD TROMBONE
GIVE ME AN OLD BATON
(*marches* C.)
BEFORE THE PARADE PASSES BY
BEFORE THE PARADE PASSES BY
(*J.G.#2 exits* R. *as J.G.#4 enters* U.L. *platform, and sings:*)

I DON'T WANT TO KNOW

(softly at first; then with growing intensity)

J.G.#4.
IF MUSIC IS NO LONGER LOVELY
IF LAUGHTER IS NO LONGER LILTING
IF LOVERS ARE NO LONGER LOVING
THEN I DON'T WANT TO KNOW

IF SUMMER IS NO LONGER CAREFREE
IF CHILDREN ARE NO LONGER SINGING
IF PEOPLE ARE NO LONGER HAPPY
THEN I DON'T WANT TO KNOW

LET ME HIDE EVERY TRUTH FROM MY EYES
WITH THE BACK OF MY HAND
LET ME LIVE IN A WORLD FULL OF LIES
WITH MY HEAD IN THE SAND

FOR MY MEMORIES ALL ARE EXCITING

MY MEMORIES ALL ARE ENCHANTED
MY MEMORIES BURN IN MY HEAD
WITH A STEADY GLOW

SO IF, MY FRIENDS
IF LOVE IS DEAD
I DON'T WANT TO KNOW
(*moves from* U.L. *platform to* D.C. *as tempo increases*)

IF MUSIC IS NO LONGER LOVELY
IF LAUGHTER IS NO LONGER LILTING
IF LOVERS ARE NO LONGER LOVING
THEN I DON'T WANT TO KNOW

IF SUMMER IS NO LONGER CAREFREE
IF CHILDREN ARE NO LONGER SINGING
IF PEOPLE ARE NO LONGER HAPPY
THEN I DON'T WANT TO KNOW

(*with more and more power*)
LET ME HIDE EVERY TRUTH FROM MY EYES
WITH THE BACK OF MY HAND
LET ME LIVE IN A WORLD FULL OF LIES
WITH MY HEAD IN THE SAND

FOR MY MEMORIES ALL ARE EXCITING
MY MEMORIES ALL ARE ENCHANTED
MY MEMORIES BURN IN MY HEAD
WITH A STEADY GLOW
(*go for it*)
SO IF, MY FRIENDS
IF LOVE IS DEAD
I DON'T WANT TO KNOW!

(*"We Need A Little Christmas" music begins as J.G.#4 moves*
U.C. *to piano. Other girls enter in the spirit of the music and*
join in the singing as indicated:)

FINALE MEDLEY

   J.G.#4.
HAUL OUT THE HOLLY

(*plus*)
  J.G.#3.
PUT UP THE TREE BEFORE MY SPIRIT FALLS
  AGAIN
(*plus*)
  J.G.#2.
FILL UP THE STOCKING
(*plus*)
  J.G.#1.
I MAY BE RUSHING THINGS, BUT
DECK THE HALLS AGAIN, NOW

(*All girls are gathered around the piano and sing short reprises:*)

  J.G.#2.
DID HE NEED A STRONGER HAND?
DID HE NEED A LIGHTER TOUCH?
WAS I SOFT OR WAS I TOUGH?
DID I GIVE ENOUGH?
DID I GIVE TOO MUCH? . . .
  J.G.#4.
HE HELD ME FOR AN INSTANT
BUT HIS ARMS FELT FELT SAFE AND STRONG
IT ONLY TAKES A MOMENT . . .
  J.G.#1.
I GOTTA GIVE MY LIFE SOME SPARKLE AND FIZZ
AND THINK A THOUGHT THAT ISN'T WRAPPED UP
  IN HIS
THE PLACE THAT I CONSIDER PARADISE IS
WHEREVER HE AIN'T!
WHEREVER HE AIN'T!
  J.G.#3.
IN FILM AFTER FILM AFTER FILM
I BETROTHED HIM
WE SNUGGLED AND SMOOCHED
AND OH GOD, HOW I LOATHED HIM
OH NELSON . . . WHAT YOUR PUTTING ME THROUGH
(*Girls pose* C. *repeating earlier deadpan sophistication.*)
  ALL.
YOU MAKE OUR BLACKEYED PEAS AND OUR GRITS,
  MAME

SEEM LIKE THE BILL OF FARE AT THE RITZ, MAME
YOU CAME, YOU SAW, YOU CONQUERED AND
ABSOLUTELY NOTHING IS THE SAME.
YOUR SPECIAL FASCINATION'LL
PROVE TO BE INSPIRATIONAL
WE THINK YOU'RE JUST SENSATIONAL . . .
(*Girls move* us. *to piano and quietly sing ad lib:*)
   ALL.
HELLO, DOLLY
WELL, HELLO, DOLLY
IT'S SO NICE TO HAVE YOU BACK WHERE YOU BELONG
YOU'RE LOOKING SWELL, DOLLY
WE CAN TELL, DOLLY
YOU'RE STILL GLOWIN'
YOU'RE STILL CROWIN'
YOU'RE STILL GOIN' STRONG . . .

(*As music changes, girls move to various areas of stage, facing
    different directions as they sing with insistent optimism:*)

I'LL BE HERE TOMORROW

   ALL.
I'LL BE HERE TOMORROW
ALIVE AND WELL AND THRIVING
I'LL BE HERE TOMORROW
MY TALENT IS SURVIVING

IF BEFORE THE DAWN
THIS FRAGILE WORLD MIGHT CRACK
SOMEONE'S GOT TO TRY TO PUT THE PIECES BACK

SO FROM BENEATH THE RUBBLE
YOU'LL HEAR A LITTLE VOICE SAY
"LIFE IS WORTH THE TROUBLE
HAVE YOU A BETTER CHOICE?"

SO LET THE SCEPTICS SAY
TONIGHT WE'RE DEAD AND GONE,
I'LL BE HERE TOMORROW
SIMPLY GOING ON
(*music double times*)

SO FROM BENEATH THE RUBBLE
YOU'LL HEAR A LITTLE VOICE SAY
"LIFE IS WORTH THE TROUBLE
HAVE YOU A BETTER CHOICE?"

SO LET THE SCEPTICS SAY
TONIGHT WE'RE DEAD AND GONE
I'LL BE HERE TOMORROW
SIMPLY GOING ON
(*All move* D.C. *and sing:*)

JERRY'S GIRLS/Reprise

ALL.
MRS. LEVI
MOTHER BURNSIDE
MABEL NORMAND
IN HER CURLS
(*All lean together for a movie-close-up pose.*)

OH THE MARQUEES
(*All indicate star portraits.*)
THEY'VE IGNITED
WE'RE ECSTATIC AND EXCITED
TO BE SOME OF
JERRY'S GIRLS

(*On final chord of music, all ladies strike their same star pose
from the opening number.*)

CURTAIN

Property & Costume List

PART I:
*Large photograph portraits of stars of Jerry Herman musicals,
  i.e. Carol Channing, Pearl Bailey, Angela Landsbury, Beatrice
  Arthur, Lucille Ball, Barbra Streisand, etc.
  4 wide-brim hats
  4 parasols
  1 "Mabel" hat and cape
  1 suitcase, 1920's vintage
  4 Santa hats
  1 16' Christmas garland
  1 silver star headband
  2 director's chairs, one marked "MACK", the other marked
      "MABEL"
  1 fedora for "Mack"
  1 rag doll for "Mabel"
  4 pairs of tap shoes
  4 straw boaters decorated in different vaudeville styles
  4 canes
  1 rubber chicken
  1 "hammer-slammer" noise maker
  1 white boa
  4 red-feathered "Dolly" headpieces
* 4 life-like cutouts of Jerry Herman dressed as a waiter
  1 American flag

PART II:
  4 character hats (Chaplin, cowboy, gangster, flapper)
  1 black scarf
  1 black bowtie
  1 black western string tie
  1 four-in-hand tie
  4 feathered turbans
  4 silver champagne glasses
  3 teacups with saucers on a tray
  3 sets of hats, gloves, shawls and pearls
  1 red pregnancy smock
  1 red cape

*   Selected 8 × 10 star photographs, plus Jerry Herman waiter
    photo available. Contact Alford Productions 104 West 70th
    St. #4-C, New York, New York 10023 for information.

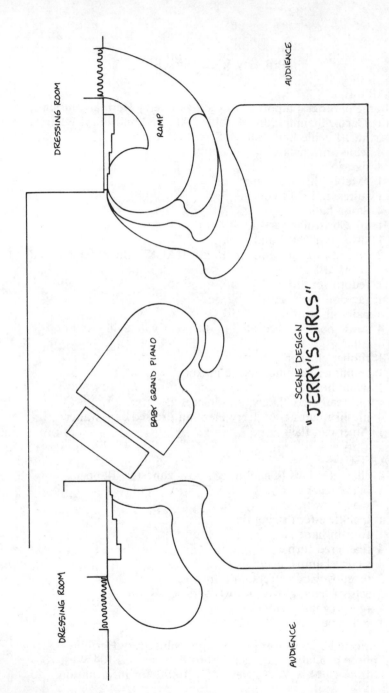

DRESSING ROOM

RAMP

AUDIENCE

DRESSING ROOM

BABY GRAND PIANO

SCENE DESIGN
"JERRY'S GIRLS"

AUDIENCE

AUDIENCE

52

Other Publications for Your Interest

TALKING WITH . . .
(LITTLE THEATRE)
By JANE MARTIN

11 women—Bare stage

Here, at last, is the collection of eleven extraordinary monologues for eleven actresses which had them on their feet cheering at the famed Actors Theatre of Louisville—audiences, critics and, yes, even jaded theatre professionals. The mysteriously pseudonymous Jane Martin is truly a "find", a new writer with a wonderfully idiosyncratic style, whose characters alternately amuse, move and frighten us always, however, speaking to us from the depths of their souls. The characters include a baton twirler who has found God through twirling; a fundamentalist snake handler, an ex-rodeo rider crowded out of the life she has cherished by men in 3-piece suits who want her to dress up "like Minnie damn Mouse in a tutu"; an actress willing to go to any length to get a job; and an old woman who claims she once saw a man with "cerebral walrus" walk into a McDonald's and be healed by a Big Mac. "Eleven female monologues, of which half a dozen verge on brilliance."—London Guardian. "Whoever (Jane Martin) is, she's a writer with an original imagination."—Village Voice. "With Jane Martin, the monologue has taken on a new poetic form, intensive in its method and revelatory in its impact."—Philadelphia Inquirer. "A dramatist with an original voice . . . (these are) tales about enthusiasms that become obsessions, eccentric confessionals that levitate with religious symbolism and gladsome humor."—N.Y. Times. *Talking With . . .* is the 1982 winner of the American Theatre Critics Association Award for Best Regional Play. (#22009)

(Royalty, $60–$40.
If individual monologues are done separately: Royalty, $15–$10.)

HAROLD AND MAUDE
(ADVANCED GROUPS—COMEDY)
By COLIN HIGGINS

9 men, 8 women—Various settings

Yes: *the Harold and Maude!* This is a stage adaptation of the wonderful movie about the suicidal 19 year-old boy who finally learns how to truly *live* when he meets up with that delightfully whacky octogenarian, Maude. Harold is the proverbial Poor Little Rich Kid. His alienation has caused him to attempt suicide several times, though these attempts are more cries for attention than actual attempts. His peculiar attachment to Maude, whom he meets at a funeral (a mutual passion), is what saves him—and what captivates us. This new stage version, a hit in France directed by the internationally-renowned Jean-Louis Barrault, will certainly delight both afficionados of the film and new-comers to the story. "Offbeat upbeat comedy."—Christian Science Monitor. (#10032)

(Royalty, $60–$40.)

FAVORITE MUSICALS from

"THE HOUSE OF PLAYS"

BALLROOM – THE BEST LITTLE
WHOREHOUSE IN TEXAS – CHICAGO –
CHRISTMAS IS COMIN' UPTOWN – THE CLUB –
DAMES AT SEA – DIAMOND STUDS –
EL GRANDE DE COCA COLA – GREASE
A HISTORY OF THE AMERICAN FILM – I LOVE
MY WIFE – I'M GETTING MY ACT TOGETHER
AND TAKING IT ON THE ROAD –
LITTLE MARY SUNSHINE – THE ME NOBODY
KNOWS – OF THEE I SING – ON THE
TWENTIETH CENTURY – PETER PAN –
PURLIE – RAISIN – RUNAWAYS – SEESAW –
SHENANDOAH – SOMETHING'S AFOOT –
STRIDER – THEY'RE PLAYING OUR SONG –
THE WIZ